Killer Ways To Make Partnerships Work For Product Managers

Techniques For Product Managers To Find Ways To Work With Others In Order To Make Their Product Successful

"Practical, proven examples of how to get the customer insights that are necessary in order to have a successful product"

Dr. Jim Anderson

Published by:
Blue Elephant Consulting
Tampa, Florida

Copyright © 2019 by Dr. Jim Anderson

All rights reserved. No part of this book may be reproduced of transmitted in any form or by any means, electronic or mechanical, including photocopying, recording or by any information storage and retrieval system without written permission of the publisher, except for inclusion of brief quotations in a review.

Printed in the United States of America

Library of Congress Control Number: 2019903060

ISBN-13: 9781090420282

Warning – Disclaimer

The purpose of this book is to educate and entertain. This book does not promise or guarantee that anyone following the ideas, tips, suggestions, techniques or strategies will be successful. The author, publisher and distributor(s) shall have neither liability nor responsibility to anyone with respect to any loss or damage caused, or alleged to be caused, directly or indirectly by the information contained in this book.

Recent Books By The Author

Product Management

- Managing Your Product Manager Career: How Product Managers Can Find And Succeed In The Right Job

- How Product Managers Can Sell More Of Their Product: Tips & Techniques For Product Managers To Better Understand How To Sell Their Product

Public Speaking

- Creating Speeches That Work: How To Create A Speech That Will Make Your Message Be Remembered Forever!

- How To Organize A Speech In Order To Make Your Point: How to put together a speech that will capture and hold your audience's attention

CIO Skills

- How CIOs Can Bring Business And IT Together: How CIOs Can Use Their Technical Skills To Help Their Company Solve Real-World Business Problems

- New IT Technology Issues Facing CIOs: How CIOs Can Stay On Top Of The Changes In The Technology That

Powers The Company

IT Manager Skills

- Killer Staffing Skills Managers Need To Know: Tips And Techniques That Managers Can Use In Order To Develop Leadership Skills

- How IT Managers Can Use New Technology To Meet Today's IT Challenges: Technologies That IT Managers Can Use In Order to Make Their Teams More Productive

Negotiating

- Killer Ways To Prepare For Your Next Negotiation: What You Need To Do BEFORE A Negotiation Starts In Order To Get The Best Possible Outcome

- Getting What You Want In A Negotiation By Learning How To Signal: How To Develop The Skill Of Effective Signaling In A Negotiation In Order To Get The Best Possible Outcome

Miscellaneous

- How To Heal A Broken Leg – Fast!: Understanding how to deal with a broken leg in order to start walking again quickly

- How Software Defined Networking (SDN) Is Going To Change Your World Forever: The Revolution In Network Design And How It Affects

Note: See a complete list of books by Dr. Jim Anderson at the back of this book.

Acknowledgements

Any book like this one is the result of years of real-world work experience. In my over 25 years of working for 7 different firms, I have met countless fantastic people and I've been mentored by some truly exceptional ones. Although I've probably forgotten some of the people who made me the person that I am today, here is my attempt to finally give them the recognition that they so truly deserve:

- Thomas P. Anderson
- Art Puett
- Bobbi Marshall
- Bob Boggs

Dr. Jim Anderson

This book is dedicated to my wife Lori. None of this would have been possible without her love and support.

Thanks for the best years of my life (so far)...!

Table Of Contents

PRODUCT MANAGERS NEED TO LEARN HOW TO MAXIMIZE PARTNERSHIPS 9

ABOUT THE AUTHOR 11

CHAPTER 1: FORCE MAJEURE: WHAT IS IT AND WHY CARE? 16

CHAPTER 2: VENDOR CONTRACTS: LET'S TALK ABOUT FORCE MAJEURE ONE MORE TIME 19

CHAPTER 3: NETFLIX TEACHES PRODUCT MANAGERS A LESSON 23

CHAPTER 4: SHOULD A PRODUCT MANAGER BE BATMAN OR THE LONE RANGER? 27

CHAPTER 5: 4 THINGS PRODUCT MANAGERS NEED TO KNOW ABOUT BUYING ANOTHER COMPANY 32

CHAPTER 6: TAYLOR SWIFT VS. SPOTIFY: A PRODUCT MANAGER PROBLEM 37

CHAPTER 7: LESSONS FOR PRODUCT MANAGERS FROM HBO 42

CHAPTER 8: PRODUCT MANAGERS GET INTO TO BUSINESS OF CHRISTMAS LASERS 47

CHAPTER 9: IS IT TIME FOR AMAZON'S PRODUCT MANAGERS TO GO BACK TO COLLEGE? 52

CHAPTER 10: PARTNERSHIPS THAT DON'T WORK OUT FOR PRODUCT MANAGERS 57

CHAPTER 11: WHAT CAN INDIA'S PAYTM MOBILE PAYMENT SYSTEM TEACH PRODUCT MANAGERS? 62

CHAPTER 12: WHY CAN'T AMAZON SELL LUXURY PRODUCTS? 69

Product Managers Need To Learn How To Maximize Partnerships

Who was it that said "It take a village..."? They may not have been talking about being a product manager, but they might as well have been. Life has become so complex that product managers can no longer make their product a success just by their own efforts. Today it takes the help of one or more partners to get your product to where it needs to be. Are you going to be ready to work with those partners?

One of the first things that product managers learn about working with partners is that we always need to have a signed contract with them. An often overlooked part of such contracts is the "force majeure" clause – product managers need to know what this really means. Product managers can learn by watching how other firms, such as Netflix, work with partners to become successful.

Product managers need to decide if they are going to be willing to work with other firms. Yes, they will be giving up some control of their product. However, like Taylor Swift and her battles with partners, they may be gaining more control over the product's success in the end.

What product managers need to realize is that not all partnerships will work out. Even at giant companies like Amazon, there will be partnerships that initially appear to be a good idea but which go bad. Learning how to use partners to tap into new markets, like India's Paytm mobile payment system has done, is the key to making your partnerships work out for you.

For more information on what it takes to be a great product manager, check out my blog, The Accidental Product Manager, at:

www.TheAccidentalPM.com

Good luck!

- Dr. Jim Anderson

About The Author

I must confess that I never set out to be a product manager. When I went to school, I studied Computer Science and thought that I'd get a nice job programming and that would be that. Well, at least part of that plan worked out!

My first job was working for Boeing on their F/A-18 fighter jet program. I spent my days programming fighter jet software in assembly language and I loved it. The U.S. government decided to save some money and went looking for other countries to sell this plane to. This put me into an unfamiliar role: I started to meet with foreign military officials in order to explain what my product did.

Time moved on and so did I. I found myself working for Siemens, the big German telecommunications company. They were making phone switches and selling them to the seven U.S. phone companies. The problem was that the switches were too complicated. Customers couldn't tell the difference between one complicated phone switch from another complicated phone switch.

The Siemens sales folks were in a bind. They didn't know enough about how the switches worked to tell their customers why they should buy them. Siemens reached out into their engineering unit looking for anyone who could help the sales teams out. I put my hand up and overnight I became a product manager.

Since then I've spent over 20 years working as a product manager for both big companies and startups. This has given me an opportunity to do everything that a product manager does many, many times. I know what works as well as what doesn't work.

I now live in Tampa Florida where I spend my time managing my consulting business, Blue Elephant Consulting, teaching college courses at the Florida Polytechnic University, and traveling to work with companies like yours to share the knowledge that I have about how product managers can make their product be a success.

I'm always available to answer questions and I can be reached at:

Dr. Jim Anderson
Blue Elephant Consulting
Email: jim@BlueElephantConsulting.com
Facebook: http://goo.gl/1TVoK
Web: **www.BlueElephantConsulting.com**

"Unforgettable communication skills that will set your ideas free..."

Create Products Your Customers Want At A Price That They Are Willing To Pay!

Dr. Jim Anderson is available to provide training and coaching on the two topics that are the most important to product managers everywhere: how do I create the products that my customers want and what should I price them at?

Dr. Anderson believes that in order to both learn and remember what he says, product managers need to laugh. Each one of his speeches is full of fun and humor so that what he says "sticks" with everyone.

Dr. Anderson's Product Management Training Includes:

1. How can you segment your market?
2. What problems are your customers having right now?
3. Which of your customer's problems does your product solve?
4. How much of this problem does your product solve?
5. How much will it cost your customer if they don't fix this problem?

Dr. Jim Anderson presents over 100 speeches per year. To invite Dr. Anderson to speak at your event, contact him at:

Phone: 813-418-6970 or
Email: jim@BlueElephantConsulting.com

Blue Elephant Consulting
Speaking. Negotiating. Managing. Marketing.

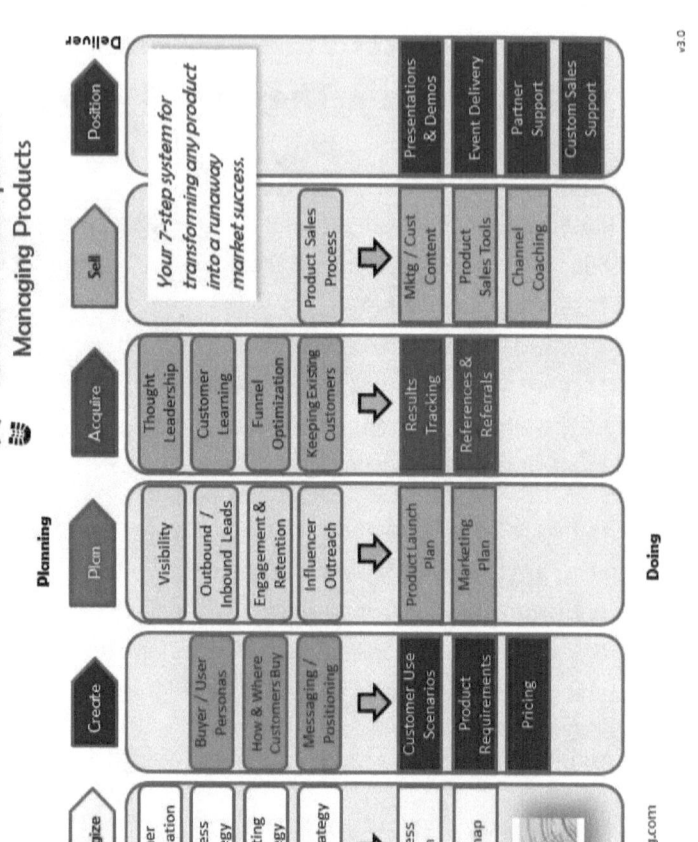

The **$TOMP** product management system has been created by **Blue Elephant Consulting** to help product managers know what to do and when to do it in order for a product to be successful.

Chapter 1

Force Majeure: What Is It and Why Care?

Chapter 1: Force Majeure: What Is It and Why Care?

While reading the Wall Street Journal last week, I happened upon a very small article that mentioned that Alcoa, the large metal processing company, had declared a force majeure on alumina (also known as aluminum oxide which is used in aluminum production) deliveries from its operation in Western Australia.

This somewhat boring legal term caught my eye because I've worked on a number of contracts that had a "force majeure" clause; however, I never really understood how or when it could be used. Well now thanks to Alcoa I know.

In Alcoa's case, there was a fire and an explosion at another company's gas-processing facility. It's going to take at least two months to repair the plant and restart the gas supply. It turns out that to process alumina and turn it into aluminum requires a lot of gas. This means that Alcoa is going to have to cut their output and therefore forced them to declare a force majeure.

What does all this talk of aluminum mean to you? If you live in Australia, it probably means that you should go buy beer and lawn chairs right NOW because prices will probably be going up. For all other product managers, this should serve as a reminder that if your product relies on another vendor, that force majeure portion of the contract is not just "contract boilerplate" — it really can be put into action.

You need to spend some time thinking about what you would do if the unthinkable happened — force majeure was declared. A backup plan/vendor is always good to have. If that's not possible, then a good P.R. campaign and working out the next steps that you would need to take with the folks in the legal department would be good to do.

Chapter 2

Vendor Contracts: Let's Talk About Force Majeure One More Time

Chapter 2: Vendor Contracts: Let's Talk About Force Majeure One More Time

We had talked about force majeure awhile back, and apparently it was interesting enough to catch the attention of one of my colleagues. Phil is a hard-charging product manager who works in the telecommunications space and he just sent me an email that was talking about another story where a vendor had to declare force majeure:

> Jim,
> Shortly after I read your posting on force majeure I saw an article that said that Royal Dutch Shell has just announced that they won't be able to meet a big piece of their Nigerian oil-export obligations for their customer for the next two months because of militant attacks on their facilities. The force majeure legally protects Shell from not meeting contractual obligations because of factors outside of its control. So much for gas prices going down anytime soon!
>
> Phil
> Senior Product Manager

During our last discussion, we spent some time making sure everyone understood what force majeure was. This time around, we should probably discuss what you need to do as a product manager if one of your vendors declares a force majeure!

This is just the tip of the business continuity planning iceberg. As product managers we are responsible for the success of our products no matter if they are just being rolled out or if they are already currently available. The wrong time to worry about the loss of a critical vendor is after something has happened. The right time is when you are introducing your product. There are three questions that you need to both ask and answer:

1. What Are All Of The Things That Could Possibly Happen: This requires a big blank sheet of paper and some serious brainstorming. Generally things fall into categories such as natural disasters, political unrest, pandemics, etc.

2. What Are The Things That Probably Might Happen: You can't plan for every possibility (your budget is not that big!). So instead you need to identify the top possibilities on your list of all things. How long your probable lists is depends on your budget and your available time.

3. Plan, Plan, Plan: You don't need separate plans for earthquakes, floods, fires, etc. Instead, you need just one plan with a few special case steps. Putting this together BEFORE you need it is the key to being a product manager who is always on top of things.

Once you have a plan, you might think that you are all done. As my friend Phil says "… a plan is just the start of the real work…" He's correct: a plan starts to go out-of-date once it's been created. You need to revisit it at least twice a year and make sure that that names, contact info, and actions are still valid.

Chapter 3

Netflix Teaches Product Managers A Lesson

Chapter 3: Netflix Teaches Product Managers A Lesson

Once upon a time, going to a Blockbuster Video store was a regular part of my weekend. Since I am *such* an engineer, running back to the store the next day to return the video that I had watched was also part of my weekend. However, I don't do any of these things any more – now that Netflix has entered my life.

Netflix blew Blockbuster Video out of the water and they did it very quickly. Instead of trying to compete with Blockbuster on their own terms, Netflix redefined the market and did away with all of those video stores. Poof! I'm sure that we can all applaud what Netflix has done so far; however, if you were a Product Manager working at Netflix, what would you be doing now?

Let's look at the facts: Netflix currently has a very successful product. However, technology keeps moving forward. This product, like so many of our products, has a limited shelf life. Netflix has a lot of existing customers. What do they need to do to retain their existing customers even while they move forward?

Right now it sure looks like the future of at-home movie watching is streaming video via the Internet. Exactly how this is going to work itself out is still just a bit unclear. So what should a Netflix product manager be doing right now? How about laying down the path to the future with the full realization that things may change on the way.

The key is to make delivery of the Netflix movies to their customers as easy as possible. I'm pretty sure that Netflix believes that the transition from mailed DVDs to watching streaming video will be a gradual process that will happen over time – not a flash cut. Netflix has been offering access to streaming video over the Internet for over a year now. Initially they limited how many hours of video each user could stream each month; however, at the start of 2008 they made this unlimited. The only downside to this service is the selection: it's pretty much movies and TV shows that have run their course. The new releases are not available here.

What's next? Allowing end users to stream video not into their laptops, but rather into their existing humongous TVs. In order to do this, Netflix needs some serious partnerships. This appears to be what the Netflix product managers are spending their time doing. Netlfix and LG Electronics have teamed up to offer a $500 Blue-ray DVD player that will also stream Netflix movies. Netflix has announced a partnership with Microsoft to allow users of Xbox live to stream Netflix movies. Finally, Netflix has worked with Roku to develop a standalone player that will allow movies to be streamed to your TV.

Which one of these partnerships is the right one? Who knows? I suspect that a lot of what is going on here is an attempt by Netflix to discover what the correct product pricing is for this new type of product. The bet is that one of these approaches will bear some fruit and will allow Netflix to remain in the lead in their market. In the end, can any Product Manger ask for anything more?

Chapter 4

Should A Product Manager Be Batman Or The Lone Ranger?

Chapter 4: Should A Product Manager Be Batman Or The Lone Ranger?

Product managers are responsible for making a lot of decisions about our products while they are being developed; however, one of the most important decisions has to be if we are going to team with another company to develop a product. It's the classic "Batman" (he's got a sidekick names Robin) vs "The Lone Ranger" type of decision. Which way should you go?

Products That Are Simple

Look, not every product out there requires rocket scientists to create (can anyone say "pet rock"?). A couple of researchers, Esteve Almirall and Ramon Casadesus-Maxanell have spent some time looking into this issue.

What they have found may surprise you. It turns out that if you decide to partner with another firm, it's going to create a whole bunch of hassles for you as a product manager. This can be just a cost of doing business; however, if the product that you are developing is simple, then partnering is a waste of your time.

The simpler the product, the less need there is to partner with another firm. Doing so will only slow down the development process as the teams try to coordinate when such collaboration really could all be done internally. Additionally, when it comes time to market the product, the firms involved may have differing opinions on how to go about doing this.

Products That Are Complicated

All the way on the other side of the product development spectrum are complex products. These are the ground-breaking products that potentially your customers have never seen before. Think of things like the original Palm Pilot or the Apple iPad.

These products are also poor candidates to be created by companies that team up. The reasons are fairly simple: ultimately during the development process the product teams are going to be looking for ways to innovate. This process is very hard to do internally and almost impossible to do if you have to coordinate your actions with an external company.

Especially if your product has no competition because it is so very new, then you know how hard it is for a product manager to keep your own management supporting the project. Just imagine how hard it would be to keep the management at multiple companies onboard!

Products That Are Just Right For Collaboration

Sorry for being so negative about this idea of companies collaborating in order to develop a new product. However, it's not all gloom and doom. It turns out that there is one class of products that actually can benefit from having a product manager bring in an outside company as a development partner: medium-low complexity products.

Why does external collaboration work here? Good question. It turns out that when the design of a product is not all that hard, but when there are decisions that can go either way, having another partner company take a look at what your company is doing can really help.

Their insights can help prevent your company from making those product decisions that always seem so foolish in hindsight. The benefit of this insight turns out to far outweigh the effort that you'll have to go through to coordinate development activities and marketing programs.

What All Of This Means For You

In our childhood we all liked both Batman and the Lone Ranger. However, when it comes to the job of a product manager we end up having to choose who we like better. The choice is not always easy to make.

If the product that we are developing is either fairly simple or wickedly complex, then partnering with another firm is a poor idea. It will just slow things down and won't provide a lot of extra value. However, if we are working on a medium-low complexity product then partnering can have valuable benefits by providing additional sets of inputs and observations.

Product managers are generally not afraid to go it alone. However, there are times that we really do need another company to act as our sidekick when we are developing a new product. It's the ability to make the right decision to partner or not that will turn you into a product management superhero within your company…

Chapter 5

4 Things Product Managers Need To Know About Buying Another Company

Chapter 5: 4 Things Product Managers Need To Know About Buying Another Company

As the global economy comes roaring back, more and more companies are discovering that their balance sheets are now loaded with cash. Their investors don't really want them to be building up stockpiles of money, instead they want the company to be growing. The quickest way for your company to do this may be to **buy another company** and add their products to your portfolio (much simpler than having to follow that product development definition thing). If your company decides to do this, what four things do you have to know about the best way to do these types of deals in order for the purchase to be a success?

Know the Business And The Industry

Why is your company all of sudden interested in buying the firm that they are considering? Did your CEO read a magazine article that told him that this was the new "hot" market or product that your company just had to get involved in? If so, then your life as a product manager may be just about ready to **become much more difficult** and that's not going to look good on your product manager resume.

What you need to do is to make sure that at least somebody in power at your company knows both the business and the industry that the firm that you are considering buying plays in. This means that your company has to either have, or at least obtain through the use of consultants, deep sector analysis, industry, or geographic strong expertise in regards to the deal that is being contemplated.

Be Skeptical About Any Growth Assumptions

Don't we all just **make up those projections about future growth**? Or if not "make up", then at least don't we have a lot of doubt about one or more of the assumptions on which such projections are based even when we are the ones making the forecast?

In a study of executives that was done by Ernst & Young, they found that most believe that purchases of other companies fail because **the top-line revenue projections didn't pan out in the end**. What this means is that the company that was doing the buying ended up overestimating the strategic value of the company that they were buying and they ended up paying too much for it. Make sure that your company looks at every forecast with a doubting eye.

Don't Let Your Company Borrow Too Much

If your company wants to buy another company, then **how is it going to pay for it?** As a product manager you should be very nervous if your company is going to be borrowing a lot of money to make this deal happen.

When a company uses a lot of leverage (borrows a lot of money), then this is going to **magnify any problems** that show up if the company that you are buying doesn't perform the way that everyone thought that it would. As a product manager, you need to make sure that your company does not take on too much financial risk in order to add to its product lines.

Make Sure That You Take Your Time After The Deal Is Done

Have you ever seen those amazing pictures of a snake just after it's eaten an egg? What they don't tell you is that the snake won't eat for days afterwards because it's going to be **too busy digesting what it just ate**.

When your company buys another company, you need to make sure that everyone realizes that **it's going to take some time to digest the new acquisition**. Don't allow people to be thinking in terms of months, instead insist that they think in terms of years. Integration of two firms is much more than just getting information systems to work together. It includes merging two cultures and people into one new firm. Make sure that you have the time that you'll need to do this correctly.

What All Of This Means For You

When your company finds itself flush with cash and has stakeholders who are demanding that the company focus on growth, it may be tempted to go out and **buy another company**. As a product manager, this may have a very large impact on the set of products that you manage even if this was never covered in your product manager job description.

In order to make sure that any acquisition turns out well for your company, you need to make sure that your company **follows 4 generally accepted principles** for how such a purchase should be done. First you need to make sure that the company fully understands the business and the industry that they are buying into. Next, you need to be skeptical about any stated growth assumptions. Make sure that your company doesn't borrow too much money to make the deal because that can cause a great deal of pressure on you later on. Finally, make sure that enough time is given to fully integrate both companies.

It turns out that buying another company and adding its staff and products to your company **can result in fantastic growth**. However, the details about how best to make this happen is where too many product managers fall down. The next time that your company is thinking about buying another company, make sure that you apply these four principles before the deal is done.

Chapter 6

Taylor Swift vs. Spotify: A Product Manager Problem

Chapter 6: Taylor Swift vs. Spotify: A Product Manager Problem

Guess what: we don't buy music any more. Nope, gone are the days that we'd go out to the store and pay US$15 for the latest album from our favorite artist. iTunes and downloadable music pretty much killed this market. However, it turns out that **something brand new has shown up** that is killing iTunes and the downloadable music market: Spotify.

Why Doesn't Taylor Swift Like Spotify?

In the brave new world of streaming music you and I no longer purchase music. Instead, what we do is we sign up for a subscription to a music streaming service. There are a number of them with names that we all recognize now: Pandora, Beats, Spotify, etc. For a fee these services will allow us to tell them what kind of music we like (Rock, Country, Soul, etc.) and they'll pick out music that matches our tastes and **create a never ending sound track for us to listen to**. Clearly this has altered the product development definition for music products.

This new form of music consumption has been growing like a weed. The RIAA reports that streaming services like Spotify grew 28% in the first-half of 2014 alone and now account for 27% of industry revenue. However, because it is brand new, this means that **all of the rules have not yet been determined** and that's why Taylor Swift is in a fight with Spotify.

So what happened here? Simply put Taylor Swift had a new album come out, 1989, and she and her record company wanted to maximize sales. Her record company talked with Spotify and asked them to limit which of their customers could listen to her new music. First they wanted only paying customers of Spotify (the ones who pay to not hear any ads) to be able to listen to her music. Next, they only wanted customers in Europe where Taylor Swift is trying to build a fan base to be able to hear her new music. Spotify said no and so **she pulled her music off of their service**.

What Should The Spotify Product Managers Do?

As a product manager, anytime a supplier is unable to provide you with the parts that you need, you've got a problem on your hands. Clearly Taylor Swift provides a product that Spotify customers enjoy. With her no longer being willing to provide that product, **this places Spotify and its product managers in a difficult position** that's not going to look good on their product manager resume. If they don't do something, then there is a good chance that at least some of their customers may leave them for other services who do have Taylor Swift products.

What these product managers are going to have to realize is that what their customer's really want is music that sounds like Taylor Swift. If they can't have the real thing, then **can they have something that sounds close?** This is where the power of playlists can come to the aid of Spotify's product managers. For you see, because subscribers leave it up to Spotify to pick what the next song that they'll listen to will be, the concept of playlists was created. A subscriber can create a playlist based on an artist or a theme and then Spotify will pick the sequence of music that matches that playlist.

Since Spotify can no longer provide Taylor Swift songs as a part of a subscriber's playlist selections, the product managers are going to have to **get creative**. They've already started doing this. Spotify has posted playlists, "A Little Playlist Poetry for Taylor Swift," and, "What to Play While Taylor's Away," including songs from Sam Hunt and Ed Sheeran, to help Swift's fans cope. I would suggest that Spotify product managers should go out and find a singer who sounds just like Taylor Swift and have that performer create covers of Taylor's songs (legally) and then substitute those songs and even new ones where they've had to pull Taylor's songs. What a great opportunity for some unknown artist!

What Does All Of This Mean For You?

As product managers, we are at the mercy of our product's suppliers. If they stop providing us with what we need to create our product, it is going to have a **big impact** on the type of product and the quantity of products that we can offer to our customers. The Spotify product managers are facing a situation like this that was never a part of their product manager job description because recording artist Taylor Swift has decided to pull her entire catalog of songs off of the Spotify service.

What this means for the Spotify product managers is that when their subscribers have playlists that include Taylor Swift songs, they won't be able to hear what they want to hear. This means that the Spotify product managers are going to have to **provide substitutes**. It might even open a door for these product managers to find an artist who sounds like Taylor Swift to create songs to fill in the gap.

When a supplier is either unwilling or unable to provide us with the parts that we need in order to create our product, **a product manager must take action**. We don't want to stop providing our product. Instead, we need to find alternatives to the supply that is no longer available. This is exactly what the Spotify product managers need to do. It appears as though they are already taking action to do this and they just might be able to create a service that can get along without Taylor Swift being a part of it.

Chapter 7

Lessons For Product Managers From HBO

Chapter 7: Lessons For Product Managers From HBO

We all know who HBO is, right? They are the premium cable television channel that even if you subscribe to cable, if you want HBO you have to pay an additional fee to get. Back in the day, HBO was the place where you could watch recent movies before they showed up in your local Blockbuster video rental store. However, now HBO is the place for great new shows like True detective, Girls, and Silicon Valley. However, more and more people are **"cutting the cord"** and dropping their cable subscriptions. What are the HBO product managers to do?

HBO's Relationship With The Cable Companies

Since it first started, HBO has had a very close relationship with the cable companies. They had to – it was the cable companies who **"owned" the end customer** and HBO relied on them to upsell the HBO service to people who had already signed up to receive cable. The cable companies relied on HBO to provide content that was only available to cable subscribers in order to get more people to sign up to receive cable.

However, then the millennials came along. These kids have decided that they can get the entertainment content that they want via the Internet and so **they no longer need to have either a telephone to their house or cable television**. The industry term for these types of non-customers is "cord cutters". Current estimates are that there are 10.5M homes in the U.S. who have only an Internet connection.

The product managers at HBO saw what was going on and said to themselves that they wanted "… to be available to their customers where, when, and how people wanted to access their service." This led to HBO changing their product development definition and creating HBO Now which is a broadband version of their product – no cable connection needed. As you can well imagine, the cable companies were none too happy about this new service from HBO which did not require their customers to have a cable connection. However, the HBO product managers pointed out to the cable companies that **they were also Internet Service Providers (ISPs)** and they were serving millions of broadband only customers who were a prime target for subscribing to the new HBO Now service. If they can make their point, then the HBO product managers will have something to add to their product manager resume.

The Future Looks Bright For HBO Now

The strategy that the HBO product managers are taking in order to get their new HBO Now service off the ground is to talk with the cable providers to see if they would like to **include this new service in their broadband only packages**. What they are trying to do is to pitch this new service as a great opportunity for traditional cable providers. Additionally, the HBO product managers are talking with non-traditional channel partners such as Apple, Android, and Roku.

The HBO product managers have studied their market. They believe that there are 10-15 million potential customers out there who want HBO but who do not currently subscribe to it. These are the people that they would like to be able to **reach with their HBO Now service**. The HBO product managers believe that cable customers no longer want 500 cable channels. Instead they want custom packages made just for them. If the cable companies start to offer this type of service, then the customer's monthly bill should decrease. When this happens, HBO believes that customers will then have the money that they'll need in order to sign up for HBO Now.

In order for HBO Now to be a success in the long run, the HBO product managers are going to have to make sure that **they can offer the programming that will cause people to keep coming**

back for more. That's why they are trying to paint HBO Now as a different sort of canvas than the traditional cable channels that everyone is used to. What they want to do is to attract the best and the brightest that Hollywood has to offer to come to them and say that they want to create something unique to be shown on HBO Now. This could consist of a series of mini-movies, comedy shows, sports, etc. If the HBO product managers can pull this off, then they will have created a product that everyone will want to subscribe to.

What All Of This Means For You

Just about everyone knows who HBO is – they provide a premium cable channel that once you subscribe to cable, you can pay even more money to get. When HBO first started out, they provided non-stop playing of recent movies. Now they've expanded their offering and provide top-notch TV shows. The HBO product managers took a look at their product manager job description and have just launched **an Internet-only service called HBO Now**. What were they thinking?

The HBO product managers realize that a big chunk of the cable TV subscriber market is transforming into the millennials. This generation of customer doesn't believe in having a phone to their house (they all have mobile phones) and they don't believe in paying for cable channels that they'll never watch. **They are being called "cord cutters"**. The HBO product managers are working with the cable companies to try to get them to offer HBO Now to their broadband only customers as part of a bigger deal. If cable customers can get smaller custom packages from their cable providers, then they'll have money to spend on HBO Now.

It appears as though the HBO product managers are doing all of the right things. They have realized that their core market is changing as more and more cable customers cut the cord. They've created an Internet only product that should appeal to those customers who only have Internet service. If they can carefully **manage their existing relationship with the cable providers**, they just might be able to have their cake and eat it too!

Chapter 8

Product Managers Get Into To Business Of Christmas Lasers

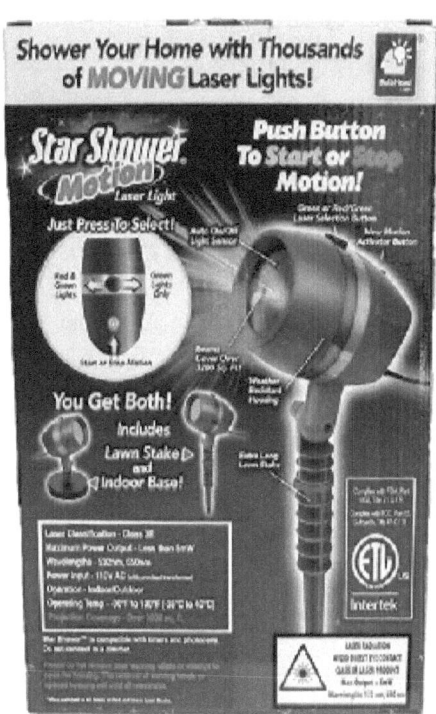

Chapter 8: Product Managers Get Into To Business Of Christmas Lasers

The Christmas season has always been the time that home owners take the time to **decorate the outside of their homes to celebrate the season**. What this generally involved was going into either the attic or the basement in order to drag out box after box that contain outside lights and decorations. Once this had been done, next came the physical challenge of putting up all of the lights and finding enough extension cords to connect them to outlets so that they could be turned on. This was a strenuous undertaking that nobody ever looked forward to. This was all before lasers got involved.

Say Hello To The Christmas Lasers

I believe that it was last year when I was walking my dogs around my neighborhood at Christmas time that I first encountered Christmas lasers. A few of the homeowners had purchased small laser projectors that looked like a normal flood light and had positioned them so that they pointed towards the house. When it got dark out, these laser projectors **displayed a brilliant collection of red and green laser dots on the house**.

The appearance was very nice. The time that it took to stick one laser projectors in the ground and turn it on was fantastic – this took much less time than crawling along your roof and hanging traditional Christmas lights took. However, last year the problem was, as told to me by one of my neighbors, was that **the laser projection system was so popular that the stores were all running out of them** – they were nowhere to be found. This problem is not going to look good on someone's product manager resume.

This year the supply problem seems to have been solved. A large number of the houses in my neighborhood were lit up by laser display systems this time around. What made things even more interesting is that the systems had been improved over what was available last year. This time around the laser lights had the ability to move and this caused the lights to dance over the face of the house and points of light could come together to make stars and then break up again. **The resulting images were very nice and very Christmas.**

The Challenge Of Keeping Your Channels Happy At Christmas

As nice as all of these Christmas laser lights were, there were some serious product manager issues going on behind the scenes. The manufacturer of the Star Shower Motion laser projection system, Telebrands Corporation has been both surprised and pleased at how popular their product has become. A part of every product manager job description is to try to sell as many copies of our product as possible. What this meant for Telebrands is that this year they were selling their product through standard retailers (Walmart, Target, etc.) **as well as online through Amazon**. This is where the problems started.

Amazon wants "… customers to come to Amazon and find the lowest prices." What this means is they have an impressive array of technology deployed to **watch what other retailers are selling a product for** so that Amazon can sell the same product at a lower price. After Thanksgiving and before Christmas, Telebrands watched their product shoot up Amazon's sales rankings list. This was great news, but their product had become the object of an online price war between the different retailers who were all offering the same product.

Telebrands offered their product to all retailers for the same wholesale price: US$30. Traditional retailers provide the bulk of Telebrands sales and Amazon only really contributes about 2%

of sales. It turns out that **Amazon's frequent online price changes are challenging retailers**. The Amazon product managers have shown that they are willing to give up profits on one item in order to attract customers whom they hope will purchase multiple items all at the same time. Amazon will lower their prices to grab more market share. What this means is that Telebrands is going to have to find ways to keep all of their channel partners happy next year.

What All Of This Means For You

It is the dream of every product manager that we create a product that has such a great product development definition that **everyone wants to get their hands on it**. The product managers at Telebrands seems to have done this when they created their Star Shower Mobile Christmas laser product. Now all they have to do is to find a way to manage their product's explosive growth.

When this product first became available last year, it was in short supply because of the overwhelming demand for it. However, this year they have enough product that they are able to sell it through traditional retailers like Walmart, Target, and Bed Bath & Beyond. This year they also started to sell the product online through Amazon. This is when they started to run into problems. Amazon was able to offer the product at a lower price than other retailers because **they were willing to generate lower profits in order to capture more customers**. This made life very difficult for the traditional retailers and they complained to Telebrands.

All product managers want to find a way to sell more of their product. The Telebrands product managers clearly have a hit on their hands right now. Next year Telebrands is going to have to find a way to **very carefully balance their different types of channels against each other**.

Chapter 9

Is It Time For Amazon's Product Managers To Go Back To College?

Chapter 9: Is It Time For Amazon's Product Managers To Go Back To College?

Let's face it, Amazon is a very big company that has done a lot of things correctly. We all know that we can visit their web site, pick out something that we want and almost magically it's going to show up at our door in just a few days. All of this success has put some pressure on the Amazon product managers. **They need to keep finding ways to allow the company to keep growing.** As product managers we all know what this means – new products. Recently the Amazon product managers decided to expand their product development definition and introduced a new product that was yanked off the market after only a couple of days. What went wrong?

Paying For School

In the world that we live in, **going to college is an expensive undertaking**. Paying for four years (at least) of schooling, books, lab materials, housing, etc. can all add up. Most students who are just starting out on this journey don't have enough savings to see them though the entire journey. What this means is that they are going to need to take some loans out now that they'll hopefully be able to pay back after they get their degree and then go out and get a job.

Students who are looking to find a way to finance their college education generally have **two options**: federal loans (from the government) and private loans (from a bank). These two types of loans are very different from each other. Federal loans are currently being offered at a historically low interest rate of 3.76% fixed (which means that the interest rate won't change). However, private loans are generally offered at much higher rates which currently could be as high as 13.74%.

The issue of just exactly how much debt a student is going to emerge from college with is a very important question. Generally speaking, student loans don't have to be paid back while the student is in school. However, once they leave school (hopefully by graduating) the payments start. Currently students owe US$1.3 trillion (yes, that's right – trillion) in student loans. More than 90% of that money is in the form of Federal loans. However, that also means that **10% of that very large number is owed to banks**.

What Was Wrong With This Product

The issue of crushing students with loans that they will never be able to repay is currently in the news. Into this charged environment **the Amazon product managers decided to step**. Amazon teamed up with the bank Wells Fargo (you remember, the bank that just got in trouble for signing people up for products that they didn't want) and planned on offering interest rate discounts on private student loans to qualified members of Amazon's new "Prime Student" service. Sure sounds like something that could be added to a product manager resume.

Almost as soon as it was announced, this new product offering **came under heavy fire**. The Institute for College Access & Success (Ticas) is a nonprofit organization that focuses on higher-education as well as student-loan issues. Ticas said that the new Amazon product was an attempt to dupe students who are eligible for federal loans into taking out more costly private loans.

Ticas did more than just voice its objections to the Amazon / Wells Fargo partnership. **They took their concerns to Capitol Hill in Washington**. There they met with influential senators who are involved in the federal student loan program. These senators then met privately with Amazon and expressed their concern with Amazon using their brand to sell private student loans and that the discount that they were offering could be cancelled or changed at any time. The Amazon product managers got the message and Amazon and Wells Fargo ended up scrapping the product that had taken over a year to create.

What All Of This Means For You

Sometimes even the best sounding product can turn out to be a dud. In the U.S., when a student wants to go to college, it's going to cost a lot of money. The product managers at Amazon saw an opportunity to create a product that would connect college bound students who use the Amazon service with discounted private college loans. **It turns out that despite what they thought their product manager job description said, this was not a good idea**.

Almost immediately after Amazon launched their new student loan matching service it started to get negative reviews. It turns out that in the U.S. students can get federal student loans with a very low interest rate. Private student loans are offered by banks and come with a much higher interest rate. Student advocacy groups were concerned that the Amazon brand would be used to **steer students** into higher priced private loans if they were not aware of the availability of federal student loans. Additionally, the Amazon deal was not all that great because the offered discounts could go away or be changed at any time.

This sure looks like a case where the Amazon product managers had their hearts in the right place, but they didn't think the product offering through all the way. It turns out that only about 10% of all student loans are private loans and the people who offer these loans are not seen as being nice people. **This is clearly one product offering that Amazon should never agreed to deliver!**

Chapter 10

Partnerships That Don't Work Out For Product Managers

Chapter 10: Partnerships That Don't Work Out For Product Managers

As a product manager, you want to be able to get your product out in front of as many potential customers as possible. However, this is something that sometimes your company can't accomplish all by themselves. When you realize this, you often start to look for a partner – somebody who can help change your product development definition and introduce you to more potential customers. This is a great idea, but these **joint marketing relationships** don't always work out...

How About Some Frequent Flyer Miles?

If you have a product that you want the world to get excited about, one marketing strategy is to **pair your product with another product that has already established itself as being popular**. The thinking here is that since people have already shown that they want the other product, if you can ride along with the other product more people will purchase your product. Hopefully after this happens, they'll use your product and fall in love with it and make more purchases in the future.

It turns out that there is a group of consumers who have **fallen in love with frequent flyer miles**. These folks collect these miles like they were made out of gold and then they use them to pay for travel to far off places that they would normally not be able to afford to go to. Since you already have people who would be willing to purchase products if somehow that purchase could result in them getting more frequent flyer miles, you have a preexisting audience for your product if you could just pair it with frequent flyer miles.

A lot of other products have done this in the past. When the U.S. mint offered free shipping on their new dollar coins in order to get them into circulation, frequent flyer hoarders ordered them using credit cards that gave them frequent flyer miles and then paid for the coins using the coins themselves. In the past cereal companies have put frequent flyer mile offers on their boxes and when they've done this, their product has flown off the shelves **often leaving them bare**. Now that's something to add to your product manager resume! Car dealerships have also offered frequent flyer miles to people who would be willing to come in and test drive a car.

What Does Love Have To Do With Frequent Flyer Miles?

If all of these other product pairings with frequent flyer miles were successful, you'd think that **perhaps they could help the sales of your product out also, right?** That is apparently the thinking that went on in the minds of the product managers at several online dating sites. The thinking was that if they could offer frequent flyer miles to new customers who signed up for their service, then they could probably attract more customers.

For what it's worth, **this appeared to be a very good idea**. The offer was that customers could get 150 frequent flyer points from British Airways for every dollar that they spent on new subscriptions to Match.com. They could also get 130 points if they signed up for eHarmony. An annual membership to Match.com costs US$215 and that meant that by just signing up a frequent flyer mile collector could gain 32,250 miles. That is a very good deal.

You know what happened here. Married people who collect frequent flyer miles started to sign up for these dating sites just to get the frequent flyer miles. It didn't take too long for the dating firms to discover what was going on and **they very quickly changed their minds**. They refunded everyone's signup fees and cancelled the frequent flyer miles that they were going to get. Apparently what had happened was that an outside firm that was tasked with getting more people to sign up for the dating sites had hatched on this plan without consulting the site owners. Lesson learned.

What All Of This Means For You

The idea behind pairing your product with a product that has already been shown to be successful is a great idea and should be a part of everyone's product manager job description. Since people already like that product, they may be willing to purchase your product just to get that product. Frequent flyer miles are very popular among the people who collect them and **pairing a product with them seems like a good idea**.

In the past there have been a number of different products that have been paired with frequent flyer miles. These have included the U.S. Mint, cereal companies, and car dealerships. **All of these have been successful programs**. Some online dating sites decided to try pairing memberships on their site with a frequent flyer mile give-away offer. It turned out that this was very, very popular – a lot of people signed up for the sites once the new offer was announced. However, as the product managers started to take a closer look at just exactly who was signing up, they didn't like what they were seeing. A large number of the people who signed up were already married and probably were not going to be using the dating website. These new members had their money returned and their frequent flyer miles cancelled.

What we need to be very careful of as product managers is that **pairing of products needs to be done carefully**. If the product that we pair our product with is too popular, it may serve to attract the wrong type of people who are really not customers for our product. That's not going to do us any good in the long run. Instead, pair your product with a complementary product and allow both companies to benefit each time a customer selects your product.

Chapter 11

What Can India's Paytm Mobile Payment System Teach Product Managers?

Chapter 11: What Can India's Paytm Mobile Payment System Teach Product Managers?

I live in the U.S. When I want to buy something, I have roughly four different options for how I can pay for it: cash, a check, credit cards, or PayPal. In India, they have traditionally only had one option: cash. In the past few years, the global credit card companies have started to arrive in India, but it has been slow going and not that many stores accept credit cards and not that many people have credit cards. This has opened the door for **online payment solutions to start to offer their services**. Paytm is one such firm and their product managers have done an excellent job of conquering the Indian payment market.

How Paytm Become So Successful

As is the case with every startup, just a short time ago Paytm didn't even exist. Paytm was launched in India in 2010. The original goal of Paytm was to **provide a mobile phone recharge and bill payments service**. When this offering took off, Paytm changed their product development definition and expanded to provide payment services for buying movie tickets and paying an electricity bill. Paytm could also be used to buy groceries or transfer money that you owed to someone.

The rapid growth of Paytm has been impressive. Currently, **over five million merchants in India accept payment using Paytm**. This becomes even more impressive when you realize that this is 5x the number that currently accept credit cards. Paytm currently has 225 million mobile wallet customers. This is 4x the number of customers that the nearest Indian mobile payment company has. All of this would look good on a product manager resume.

Paytm was just another online payment system in the early days. However, then Uber, the ride sharing application, came to

India. The company got into a disagreement in 2014 with India's central bank who put restrictions how they were going to accept credit card payments. Paytm approached Uber and **offered to allow their customers to use Paytm's mobile wallet as a way of getting around the problem that they were having with using credit cards**. This allowed Paytm to capture a new group of tech savvy consumers.

Challenges That Paytm Faces Going Forward

India is a very, very large country. What this means for the Paytm product managers is that they are going to be **facing a number of big challenges as they go forward**. One of the biggest challenges is that they are not the only Indian startup that is trying to attract customers to use their online payment system. Other competitors include the firms MobiKwik and FreeCharge. In addition, Samsung has just launched their Samsung Pay in India. Additionally, other popular mobile applications such as WhatsApp are also thinking about launching online payment services.

One big challenge that Paytm may be facing in the future will be coming from **the Indian government**. The government has launched mobile payments system. This allows users to transfer money between user's bank accounts. Once again, since there are so many people in India, there will probably always be enough people to keep all of the competitors to Paytm in business and competing with Paytm.

The Indian financial system has been undergoing some significant changes lately and these can both help and harm Paytm. The Indian government has decided to take steps in order to both cut corruption and do a better job of collecting taxes from citizens. In order to make this happen, the Indian government **cancelled 86% of the currency that was in circulation**. Paytam hopes that this move will cause people to start to stop using cash and start to use the Paytm service to make purchases.

What All Of This Means For You

The Indian market is very, very large and very, very diverse. Attempting to create a product that will succeed in this market is a huge challenge for any product manager. The company Paytm has decided that it wants to compete with cash in India to become **the most popular way to complete sales transactions**. It has a good start, but the Paytm product managers are going to have to take a good look at their product manager job description because they still face a number of challenges.

Paytm is a brand new company – it was started in 2010. It started out as a way to pay your mobile phone bill and has grown into an application that can be used to pay for just about anything. The company has millions of users and over 5 million stores that support using it to make payments. Paytm was just another online payment company until they partnered with Uber in order to make paying for rides easy to do. Paytm faces challenges in dealing with other companies in India who are **competing for the same customers**. The biggest of these competitors may turn out to be the Indian government who has also launched their own mobile payment application. The changes that the Indian government has been making to its currency may turn out to drive more people to making payments using online services.

The Paytm product managers have done an excellent job of getting their online payment service started in India. Now that they have reached a good size, **the types of challenges that they are facing will start to change**. They are going to have to deal with new competitors and find out how to retain all of the customers that they have already been able to gain. India is such a large market that there is a great deal of potential for Paytm to turn into a very large success!

Chapter 12

Why Can't Amazon Sell Luxury Products?

Chapter 12: Why Can't Amazon Sell Luxury Products?

As we all know, Amazon sells a lot of different things. However, there is one area where they are distinctly lacking in products to sell: **luxury goods**. It's not as though the Amazon product managers have not held discussions with the Swatch, Gucci, LVMH Louis Vuitton, and other luxury vendors. However, so far they have not been able to reach an agreement with them. Perhaps the Amazon product managers are going to have to change their product development definition. What's up?

The Problem With Luxury Goods

So what's the big deal here? Doesn't everyone want to have their products carried in the world's biggest online store? The problem that Amazon is running into is that the world's luxury brands are saying that Amazon's online marketplace undermines the strict controls that the luxury brands believe are key to their ability to make their products exclusive – and keeping their prices high. Yes, some luxury brands have joined with Amazon in order to get their products listed on the site; however, **the really big names are all currently sitting on the sidelines**. That's not going to look good on anyone's product manager resume.

The fact that they don't currently carry any high-end goods on their site has created problems for the Amazon product managers. Amazon, the company, would very much like to find a way for them to be **a significant force in the fashion industry**. Amazon has been working to make this happen for years with very little to show for their efforts. There are very few luxury goods available on the Amazon website right now. Amazon wants to sell luxury goods because it will help to boost their margins and it will build loyalty with their higher margin Amazon Prime customers.

The Amazon product managers have not been idle. Instead, they have been spending their time **investing in the fashion industry**. One of the things that they have done is to open a very large fashion photo studio which is located in Brooklyn, New York City. Additionally, they have started Amazon's own private label brands. In order to get the word out about what Amazon is doing in the fashion market, they have sponsored events such as the Met Ball which was held at New York's Metropolitan Museum of Art. A portion of the Amazon web site has been turned into a luxury goods storefront in order to attract customers who might be looking for high-end brands.

How Amazon Is Going To Solve Their Luxury Goods Problem

The big problem that the luxury brands have with Amazon is that the small sellers who use the Amazon platform to sell their products **may be selling knock-off or counterfeit luxury items**. Amazon has dealt with this issue before. They have been able to convince some of the biggest lifestyle companies to sell their products on Amazon by promising to take action against unauthorized retailers. As an example of what Amazon has been able to accomplish, Nike has agreed to make some of their products available in the Amazon store. In order to make this happen, the Amazon product managers had to agree to do some policing of their web site and look for fakes. However, so far Amazon has only been willing to do this for the largest brands.

The Amazon product managers are facing a real dilemma here. The product managers do want to stop the sale of counterfeit goods on the Amazon site. However, what they don't want to do is to stop **legitimate goods from being sold outside of the limited distribution channels that the luxury goods manufactures want to impose on the world**. The third party sellers who are offering these goods are partially responsible for

Amazon's ability to keep prices low. It the sales of these legitimate low cost goods that Amazon doesn't want the luxury goods manufactures to interfere with.

Amazon is not taking the problem of counterfeit goods lying down. In order to be able to attract more luxury brands to the site, **Amazon has implemented a system** that constantly scans and blocks attempts to list counterfeit goods. Amazon has also implemented a program that requires third party providers who want to sell goods on the Amazon site to produce paperwork that shows that they legitimately purchased the products that they will be selling. In order to help make the luxury manufacturers more comfortable using the Amazon site, the Amazon product managers are willing to give these companies access to special tools that allow them to search both text and images on the site and permit them some control over listings on the site.

What All Of This Means For You

The product managers at Amazon have a problem on their hands that is not covered in their product manager job description. For all of the products that the world's largest online store has to offer, the one area where products are conspicuously missing is **the luxury goods area**. The Amazon product managers have been trying to reach agreements with the big luxury brands over the past few years, but they just have not been able to do it.

The problem that the Amazon product managers have been running into has to do with **counterfeits and knock-offs**. The luxury brands want Amazon to become aggressive and prevent any third party resellers from offering these goods. Although Amazon is willing to take action against anyone who is offering counterfeit goods, they are unwilling to take action against people who are selling legitimate products through non-traditional channels. Amazon has gone ahead and implemented a system that scans what is on their shelves looking for counterfeit goods. Additionally, they are willing to make their counterfeit hunting tools available to luxury goods manufacturers.

The Amazon product managers have to find a way to meet the needs of the luxury goods manufacturers if they want to have any hope of being able to sell their goods on the Amazon website. These manufactures do want to gain access to Amazon's customers, but they also want to make sure that their products **remain "special" and that they can continue to charge high prices**. There is a bridge between these two worlds. The Amazon product managers are going to have to either find this bridge or build it themselves.

It's from the forge of failure that the steel of success is formed.

Hard Work Does Not Guarantee Success, But Success Does Not Happen Without Hard Work.

- Dr. Jim Anderson

Create Products Your Customers Want At A Price That They Are Willing To Pay!

Dr. Jim Anderson is available to provide training and coaching on the two topics that are the most important to product managers everywhere: how do I create the products that my customers want and what should I price them at?

Dr. Anderson believes that in order to both learn and remember what he says, product managers need to laugh. Each one of his speeches is full of fun and humor so that what he says "sticks" with everyone.

Dr. Anderson's Product Management Training Includes:

1. How can you segment your market?
2. What problems are your customers having right now?
3. Which of your customer's problems does your product solve?
4. How much of this problem does your product solve?
5. How much will it cost your customer if they don't fix this problem?

Dr. Jim Anderson presents over 100 speeches per year. To invite Dr. Anderson to speak at your event, contact him at:

Phone: 813-418-6970 or
Email: jim@BlueElephantConsulting.com

Photo Credits:

Cover - Photo by Julia Caesar on Unsplash
https://unsplash.com/photos/3VmiRM4vW2Y

Chapter 1 – Albert
https://www.flickr.com/photos/campra/

Chapter 2 - Daniel Lobo
https://www.flickr.com/photos/daquellamanera/

Chapter 3 - Paulo O
https://www.flickr.com/photos/brownpau/

Chapter 4 - Paul Campbell
https://www.flickr.com/photos/kemitix/

Chapter 5 - nathan Esguerra
https://www.flickr.com/photos/ke_netan_to/

Chapter 6 - Scott Beale
https://www.flickr.com/photos/laughingsquid/

Chapter 7 – JasonParis
https://www.flickr.com/photos/jasonparis/

Chapter 8 – Amazon
https://www.amazon.com/Shower-Motion-Laser-Lights-Projector/dp/B01GOQNXQG

Chapter 9 – Canonicalized
https://www.flickr.com/photos/141573413@N04/

Chapter 10 - Always Shooting
https://www.flickr.com/photos/alwaysshooting/

Chapter 11 - amyjohn cse
https://www.flickr.com/photos/144481250@N05/

Chapter 12 - Tim Li
https://www.flickr.com/photos/29425486@N03/

Other Books By The Author

Product Management

- How Product Managers Can Sell More Of Their Product: Tips & Techniques For Product Managers To Better Understand How To Sell Their Product

- How Product Managers Can Sell More Of Their Product: Tips & Techniques For Product Managers To Better Understand How To Sell Their Product

- How To Create A Successful Product That Customers Will Want: Techniques For Product Managers To Boost Product Sales And Increase Customer Satisfaction

- What Product Managers Need To Know About World-Class Product Development: How Product Managers Can Create Successful Products

- How Product Managers Can Learn To Understand Their Customers: Techniques For Product Managers To Better Understand What Their Customers Really Want

- Product Management Secrets: Techniques For Product Managers To Boost Product Sales And Increase Customer Satisfaction

- Product Development Lessons For Product Managers: How Product Managers Can Create Successful Products

- Customer Lessons For Product Managers: Techniques For Product Managers To Better Understand What Their Customers Really Want

- Product Failure Lessons For Product Managers: Examples Of Products That Have Failed For Product Managers To Learn From

- Communication Skills For Product Managers: The Communication Skills That Product Managers Need To Know How To Use In Order To Have A Successful Product

- How To Have A Successful Product Manager Career: The Things That You Need To Be Doing TODAY In Order To Have A Successful Product Manager Career

- Product Manager Product Success: How to keep your product on track and make it become a success

Public Speaking

- Creating Speeches That Work: How To Create A Speech That Will Make Your Message Be Remembered Forever!

- How To Organize A Speech In Order To Make Your Point: How to put together a speech that will capture and hold your audience's attention

- Changing How You Speak To Overcome Your Fear Of Speaking: Change techniques that will transform a speech into a memorable event

- Delivering Excellence: How To Give Presentations That Make A Difference: Presentation techniques that will transform a speech into a memorable event

- Tools Speakers Need In Order To Give The Perfect Speech: What tools to use to create your next speech so that your message will be remembered forever!

- How To Create A Speech That Will Be Remembered

- Secrets To Organizing A Speech For Maximum Impact: How to put together a speech that will capture and hold your audience's attention

- How To Become A Better Speaker By Changing How You Speak: Change techniques that will transform a speech into a memorable event

- How To Give A Great Presentation: Presentation techniques that will transform a speech into a memorable event

- How To Rehearse In Order To Give The Perfect Speech: How to effectively rehearse your next speech to that your message be remembered forever!

- Secrets To Creating The Perfect Speech: How to create a speech that will make your message be remembered forever!

- Secrets To Organizing The Perfect Speech: How to organize the best speech of your life!

- Secrets To Planning The Perfect Speech: How to plan to give the best speech of your life

- How To Show What You Mean During A Presentation: How to use visual techniques to transform a speech into a memorable event

CIO Skills

- How CIOs Can Bring Business And IT Together: How CIOs Can Use Their Technical Skills To Help Their Company Solve Real-World Business Problems

- New IT Technology Issues Facing CIOs: How CIOs Can Stay On Top Of The Changes In The Technology That Powers The Company

- Keeping The Barbarians Out: How CIOs Can Secure Their Department and Company: Tips And Techniques For CIOs To Use In Order To Secure Both Their IT Department And Their Company

- What CIOs Need To Know In Order To Successfully Manage An IT Department: Decision Making Skills That Every CIO Needs To Have In Order To Be Able To Make The Right Choices

- Becoming A Powerful And Effective Leader: Tips And Techniques That IT Managers Can Use In Order To Develop Leadership Skills

- CIO Secrets For Growing Innovation: Tips And Techniques For CIOs To Use In Order To Make Innovation Happen In Their IT Department

- Your Success As A CIO Depends On How Well You Communicate: Tips And Techniques For CIOs To

Use In Order To Become Better Communicators

- What CIOs Need To Know About Working With Partners: Techniques For CIOs To Use In Order To Be Able To Successfully Work With Partners

- Critical CIO Management Skills: Decision Making Skills That Every CIO Needs To Have In Order To Be Able To Make The Right Choices

- How CIOs Can Make Innovation Happen: Tips And Techniques For CIOs To Use In Order To Make Innovation Happen In Their IT Department

- CIO Communication Skills Secrets: Tips And Techniques For CIOs To Use In Order To Become Better Communicators

- Managing Your CIO Career: Steps That CIOs Have To Take In Order To Have A Long And Successful Career

- CIO Business Skills: How CIOs can work effectively with the rest of the company!

IT Manager Skills

- Killer Staffing Skills Managers Need To Know: Tips And Techniques That Managers Can Use In Order

To Develop Leadership Skills

- How IT Managers Can Use New Technology To Meet Today's IT Challenges: Technologies That IT Managers Can Use In Order to Make Their Teams More Productive

- How To Build High Performance IT Teams: Tips And Techniques That IT Managers Can Use In Order To Develop Productive Teams

- Save Yourself, Save Your Job – How To Manage Your IT Career: Secrets That IT Managers Can Use In Order To Have A Successful Career

- Growing Your CIO Career: How CIOs Can Work With The Entire Company In Order To Be Successful

- How IT Managers Can Make Innovation Happen: Tips And Techniques For IT Managers To Use In Order To Make Innovation Happen In Their Teams

- Staffing Skills IT Managers Must Have: Tips And Techniques That IT Managers Can Use In Order To Correctly Staff Their Teams

- Secrets Of Effective Leadership For IT Managers: Tips And Techniques That IT Managers Can Use In

Order To Develop Leadership Skills

- IT Manager Career Secrets: Tips And Techniques That IT Managers Can Use In Order To Have A Successful Career

- IT Manager Budgeting Skills: How IT Managers Can Request, Manage, Use, And Track Their Funding

- Secrets Of Managing Budgets: What IT Managers Need To Know In Order To Understand How Their Company Uses Money

Negotiating

- Killer Ways To Prepare For Your Next Negotiation: What You Need To Do BEFORE A Negotiation Starts In Order To Get The Best Possible Outcome

- Getting What You Want In A Negotiation By Learning How To Signal: How To Develop The Skill Of Effective Signaling In A Negotiation In Order To Get The Best Possible Outcome

- Exploring How To Get The Deal That You Want In A Negotiation: How To Develop The Skill Of Exploring What Is Possible In A Negotiation In Order To Reach The Best Possible Deal

- Use The Power Of Arguing To Win Your Next Negotiation: How To Develop The Skill Of Effective Arguing In A Negotiation In Order To Get The Best Possible Outcome

- Learn How To Signal In Your Next Negotiation: How To Develop The Skill Of Effective Signaling In A Negotiation In Order To Get The Best Possible Outcome

- Learn The Skill Of Exploring In A Negotiation: How To Develop The Skill Of Exploring What Is Possible In A Negotiation In Order To Reach The Best Possible Deal

- Learn How To Argue In Your Next Negotiation: How To Develop The Skill Of Effective Arguing In A Negotiation In Order To Get The Best Possible Outcome|

- How To Open Your Next Negotiation: How To Start A Negotiation In Order To Get The Best Possible Outcome

- Preparing For Your Next Negotiation: What You Need To Do BEFORE A Negotiation Starts In Order To Get The Best Possible Deal

- Learn How To Package Trades In Your Next Negotiation

- All Good Things Come To An End: How To Close A Negotiation - How To Develop The Skill Of Closing In Order To Get The Best Possible Outcome From A Negotiation

- Take No Prisoners In Your Next Negotiation: How To Start A Negotiation In Order To Get The Best Possible Outcome

Miscellaneous

- How To Heal A Broken Leg – Fast!: Understanding how to deal with a broken leg in order to start walking again quickly

- How Software Defined Networking (SDN) Is Going To Change Your World Forever: The Revolution In Network Design And How It Affects You

- The Power Of Virtualization: How It Affects Memory, Servers, and Storage: The Revolution In Creating Virtual Devices And How It Affects You

- The Internet-Enabled Successful School District Superintendent: How To Use The Internet To Boost

Parental Involvement In Your Schools

- Power Distribution Unit (PDU) Secrets: What Everyone Who Works In A Data Center Needs To Know!

- Making The Jump: How To Land Your Dream Job When You Get Out Of College!

- How To Use The Internet To Create Successful Students And Involved Parents

Techniques For Product Managers To Find Ways To Work With Others In Order To Make Their Product Successful

> This book has been written with one goal in mind – to show you how to find out what your customers really want from your product. We're going to show you how to listen to what your customers are really telling you.
>
> **Let's Make Your Product A Success!**

What You'll Find Inside:

- **FORCE MAJEURE: WHAT IS IT AND WHY CARE?**

- **4 THINGS PRODUCT MANAGERS NEED TO KNOW ABOUT BUYING ANOTHER COMPANY**

- **NETFLIX TEACHES PRODUCT MANAGERS A LESSON**

- **PARTNERSHIPS THAT DON'T WORK OUT FOR PRODUCT MANAGERS**

Dr. Jim Anderson brings his 4 college degrees coupled with over 25 years of real-world experience to this book. He's managed products at some of the world's largest firms as well as at start-ups. He's going to show you what you need to do in order to make your career a success!

www.ingramcontent.com/pod-product-compliance
Lightning Source LLC
Chambersburg PA
CBHW030017190526
45157CB00016B/3069